Money Mind-Shift:

Unlocking Financial Freedom

Veiled V.

To my sister, Marisa, whose unwavering passion for personal finance and abundance mentality has inspired me to share this knowledge with others. Thank you for your support This book is dedicated to you.

To my supportive friend. Esau: Thank you for always being there for me and encouraging me to pursue my dreams. This book is a testament to your unwavering support and friendship.

Table of Contents

Introduction:
The Importance of
Attracting Money and
Financial Freedom

Money Mind-Shift: Unlocking Financial Freedom

Today, financial stability and security are critical components of a comfortable life. Money impacts everything from our health and happiness to our relationships and career choices. This book aims to delve into the intricacies of attracting money and achieving financial freedom, providing readers with practical strategies to develop a wealth consciousness, build an investment strategy, create passive income streams, and ultimately achieve financial independence.

The first chapter of this book will explore our relationship with money, including our mindset and limiting beliefs. This will discuss how to shift our mindset towards a positive and abundance-based outlook towards money, as understanding your relationship with money which is the first step towards attracting abundance into your life.

Introduction

In chapter two, we will discuss the Law of Attraction and how to use this powerful tool to manifest financial abundance. You'll learn how your thoughts and beliefs can affect your ability to attract wealth and how to use the Law of Attraction to create a positive and abundant financial reality.

Chapters three and four of this book will provide practical strategies for attracting money, including building a wealth consciousness, developing an investment strategy, and creating passive income streams. Building a wealth consciousness is about shifting your focus from scarcity to abundance and attracting wealth into your life. Developing an investment strategy is about making wise financial decisions that will help you grow your wealth over time, while creating passive income streams which is about generating income without actively trading your time for money.

Finally, chapter five will guide you through the steps to achieving financial freedom and maintaining financial independence. You'll learn how to create a financial plan that works for you and how to achieve your financial goals over time.

It's important to note that this book is a comprehensive guide to attracting money and achieving financial freedom. To achieve lasting change and success, it's crucial to read the book entirely and apply the principles outlined in each chapter. Hopefully this will provide you with

Introduction

valuable insights and practical tips to attract money

and create a life of abundance and financial

freedom.

Chapter 1: Understanding Your Relationship with Money

Money plays a crucial role in our lives, and the way we perceive and relate to it can significantly influence our financial success. In this chapter, we will delve into three vital aspects of comprehending our relationship with money: our money mindset, limiting beliefs, and the psychology of wealth creation. We will examine how our upbringing, experiences, and environment shape our money mindset, which is our overall attitude and belief system about money.

Additionally, we will look at how negative thoughts or attitudes can limit our financial success and the importance of identifying and challenging these limiting beliefs. Finally, we will explore the internal and external factors that contribute to wealth creation, such as having a positive mindset, taking risks, and recognizing opportunities.

Understanding these critical components can help

us create a more positive and abundant

relationship with money and achieve financial

freedom.

Examining Your Money Mindset:

Your money mindset is like a pair of glasses that you wear to view the world of finance. If your glasses are foggy or scratched, your vision will be limited, and you'll miss out on opportunities. To get a clear view, you need to start by assessing your beliefs about money. Ask yourself if you view money as a scarce resource or as an abundant one. Your beliefs about money can influence your actions, so it's essential to develop a positive money mindset.

For instance, if you think money is scarce, you might feel the need to hoard your cash or avoid taking financial risks. However, if you believe that there is an abundance of wealth available to you, you'll be more open to taking risks and exploring new opportunities.

Identifying Limiting Beliefs:

Limiting beliefs are like weeds that grow in your financial garden and stop your money tree from blossoming. They're sneaky and can be hard to spot, but once you identify them, you can pluck them out by their roots. Some common limiting beliefs about money include "money is the root of all evil" or "rich people are greedy." These beliefs can hold you back from achieving financial success, so it's crucial to identify and challenge them.

For instance, if you believe that money is evil, you might feel guilty about making money or feel that you're not worthy of financial success. Similarly, if you believe that rich people are greedy, you might subconsciously sabotage your efforts to accumulate wealth.

The Psychology of Wealth Creation:

Wealth creation is like a puzzle that requires all the right pieces to fit together. One of the most important pieces is the psychology behind money and success. The psychology of wealth creation encompasses having a positive mindset, being willing to take risks, and having the ability to see opportunities where others see obstacles. It's essential to understand that wealth creation is not just about external factors but also internal ones, such as beliefs and attitudes.

Such as, if you have a positive mindset and believe that success is possible, you'll be more willing to take financial risks and explore new opportunities. Similarly, if you can see opportunities where others see obstacles, you'll be able to create wealth even in challenging economic times.

In summary, examining your money mindset, identifying limiting beliefs, and understanding the psychology of wealth creation are all critical for achieving financial freedom. Think of it as the foundation for building your financial house. With a solid foundation, you can build a life of abundance and independence. However, remember that these are just examples, and it's essential to do thorough research and seek professional advice before making any financial decisions. And don't forget to have fun along the way! Financial success is a journey, not a destination.

Here is an affirmation for understanding

your relationship with money:

"I am worthy of financial abundance, and I choose to cultivate a healthy relationship with money. I approach my finances with a positive and proactive mindset, understanding that money is simply a tool to help me achieve my goals and live the life I desire. I am mindful of my spending habits and make intentional choices to align my financial decisions with my values and priorities. I trust in my ability to create a prosperous and fulfilling life for myself, and I am grateful for the abundance that flows to me through my healthy relationship with money."

Chapter 2:
The Law of Attraction and Money

The Law of Attraction is a powerful concept that has gained popularity in the field of personal development. This principle suggests that our thoughts and emotions could attract experiences and circumstances into our lives. By focusing our energy on our goals and desires, we can manifest them into reality. In this chapter, we will explore how the Law of Attraction can be applied to money and financial abundance. By cultivating a positive mindset and taking inspired action, we can attract wealth and prosperity into our lives.

Additionally, we will provide real-life examples of individuals who have successfully used the Law of Attraction to achieve financial success. These examples demonstrate the power of this principle and serve as

Chapter 2: The Law of Attraction and Money

inspiration for those seeking to create financial

abundance in their own lives.

What is the Law of Attraction?

The Law of Attraction is like Tinder for the universe. It's based on the principle that like attracts like. When we focus on positive thoughts and emotions, we will attract positive experiences and circumstances into our lives. When we focus on negative thoughts and emotions, we'll attract negative experiences and circumstances. So, instead of swiping left or right, we need to swipe up, towards the stars!

Applying the Law of Attraction to money requires cultivating a positive mindset and visualizing yourself already having the financial abundance you desire. This includes creating a vision board or writing affirmations that reinforce your belief in your ability to attract wealth. It is also crucial to take inspired action towards your financial goals, such as starting a business, investing in stocks or real estate, or negotiating a higher salary.

How to Apply the Law of Attraction to Money

To apply the Law of Attraction to money, we need to stop being a Debbie Downer and start being a Positive Polly. This means cultivating a positive mindset and visualizing ourselves already having the financial abundance we desire. So, grab some scissors and glue, and start making that vision board! It's also important to take inspired action towards our financial goals. And no, sitting on the couch eating Cheetos does not count as inspired action. It is so crucial to take inspired action towards your financial goals, such as starting a business, investing in stocks or real estate, or negotiating a higher salary. We'll discuss more on inspired action later.

Manifesting Financial Abundance

Manifesting financial abundance is the process of using the Law of Attraction to attract wealth, prosperity, and financial success into your life. This involves aligning your thoughts, emotions, and actions with the belief that you already have the financial abundance that you desire. To manifest financial abundance, you need to identify and clarify your financial goals, focus on abundance and prosperity, visualize yourself having achieved your goals, and take practical steps towards them. Cultivating a positive abundant mindset and taking inspired action are crucial components of manifesting financial abundance.

Remember, manifesting financial abundance is like being a magician, but without the hat and wand.

It's the process of using the Law of Attraction to attract wealth, prosperity, and financial success into our lives. This involves aligning our thoughts, emotions, and actions with the belief that we already have the financial abundance that we desire. It's like telling the universe, "Hey, I'm ready for my close-up!"

Many successful individuals have applied the Law of Attraction to manifest financial abundance. Oprah Winfrey is an example of someone who has openly spoken about using visualization techniques to achieve her success. She has also emphasized the importance of cultivating a positive mindset and acting towards your goals. (Oprah Winfrey: "The Oprah Winfrey Show." Youtube. 2019)

Chapter 2: The law of Attraction and Money

Jim Carrey, when he was broke and struggling as an actor, wrote himself a check for $10 million and visualized himself achieving that goal. (Jim Carrey: "Jim Carrey Shares His Inspiring Vision Board Story!" Youtube.2021) He eventually achieved financial success beyond his wildest dreams.

Bob Proctor, a well-known personal development coach, is another example of someone who has spoken extensively about the power of visualization and the Law of Attraction in achieving financial success. (Bob
Proctor: "The Science of Getting Rich Bob Proctor" YouTube.2018)

Lastly, applying the Law of Attraction to money requires cultivating a positive mindset, visualizing financial abundance, and taking inspired action. Individuals who have successfully used this principle to achieve wealth serve as inspiration and provide evidence that the Law of Attraction can be a powerful tool for creating financial abundance.

Here's an affirmation for the law of attraction

and money:

"I am a magnet for financial abundance, and I attract wealth and prosperity into my life with ease. I trust in the universe to provide me with unlimited opportunities to create abundance and manifest my financial goals. I release any limiting beliefs or negative thoughts about money, and instead, focus on the abundance and prosperity that surrounds me. I am grateful for the wealth that flows to me effortlessly and for the joy and freedom that financial abundance provides in my life."

Chapter 3:
Practical Strategies for
Attracting Money

Money can be a fickle thing, but it doesn't have to be. Here, we'll explore practical strategies for attracting money and developing a positive relationship with wealth. These strategies include building a wealth consciousness, developing an abundance mentality, and taking inspired action. Don't worry, we won't ask you to dance under the moonlight naked holding a bag of money.

Building a Wealth Consciousness:

Building a wealth consciousness involves developing a positive attitude towards money and abundance. It's like making a salad, but instead of greens, you use positive affirmations and beliefs. It involves recognizing that money is a tool that can be used to create a life of freedom and fulfillment. So, don't treat money like a bad ex, treat it like your personal chauffeur. One way to build a wealth consciousness is to focus on the abundance that already exists in your life. For example, you may be grateful for having a roof over your head, a job that pays the bills, or a supportive network of friends and family. By focusing on abundance, you can shift your mindset towards wealth creation.

Developing an Abundance Mentality:

Developing an abundance mentality involves recognizing that there is enough wealth and abundance to go around. Think of wealth like a buffet - there's enough food for everyone. It involves believing that there are always opportunities to create wealth, and that abundance is not limited. One way to develop an abundance mentality is to surround yourself with people who have a positive attitude towards money and abundance. You may also want to read books or listen to podcasts about wealth creation to expand your mindset. So, put on your earphones and let the money gurus whisper sweet nothings in your ear.

Taking Inspired Action:

Taking inspired action involves taking practical steps towards creating financial abundance. It's like going on a treasure hunt - you need a map and a shovel. It involves identifying opportunities and acting towards achieving your financial goals. For example, you may want to start a side business, invest in the stock market, or negotiate a higher salary at work. Taking inspired action requires a combination of mindset and practical skills. So, put on your thinking cap and grab your tool kit.

To conclude, developing a positive relationship with money requires a combination of mindset and practical strategies. By building a wealth consciousness, developing an abundance mentality, and taking inspired action, you can attract wealth and create a life of

financial freedom and abundance. Just remember, money

can't buy happiness, but it can buy a lot of things that

make you happy.

Here's an affirmation for practical strategies

for attracting money:

"I am open and receptive to practical strategies for attracting money into my life. I am committed to taking positive action towards my financial goals and creating a life of abundance. I trust my instincts and make wise financial decisions that align with my values and priorities. I am resourceful and creative in finding new ways to generate income and build wealth. I attract abundance and prosperity through my hard work, dedication, and willingness to learn and grow. I am grateful for the opportunities that come my way and for the financial abundance that I am creating in my life."

Chapter 4:
Building Wealth through Investing

Investing is a crucial aspect of accumulating long-term wealth and securing financial independence. This chapter delves into the fundamental principles of investing, such as developing an investment strategy and creating passive income streams. The concept of investing is simple: it involves putting your money into assets that have the potential to increase in value over time, such as stocks, bonds, mutual funds, real estate, and more. By understanding financial concepts such as diversification, asset allocation, and risk management, you can make informed decisions about your investments. Developing an investment strategy involves identifying your financial goals, risk tolerance, and investment timeline. Creating passive income streams involves generating income without actively working for it.

<u>Understanding the Basics of Investing</u>:

Investing involves putting your money into assets that have the potential to increase in value over time. These assets can include stocks, bonds, mutual funds, real estate, and more. It's important to understand the potential risks and rewards of each investment before making any decisions. It's also essential to have a basic understanding of financial concepts, such as diversification, asset allocation, and risk management.

For instance, let's say you invest $10,000 in a stock mutual fund. Over the next year, the value of the mutual fund increases by 10%, and your investment is now worth $11,000. If you sell your investment at this point, you would have earned a 10% return on your investment. However, if the value of the mutual fund decreases by 10%,

your investment would be worth $9,000, and

you would have lost 10% of your investment.

Developing an Investment Strategy:

Developing an investment strategy involves identifying your financial goals, risk tolerance, and investment timeline. For example, if you have a long- term investment horizon, you may choose to invest in stocks or real estate, which have the potential for higher returns over time. If you have a lower risk tolerance, you may choose to invest in bonds or other fixed-income assets that have lower potential returns but are more stable.

Perhaps, if your financial goal is to save for retirement, you may choose to invest in a diversified portfolio of stocks, bonds, and mutual funds. You may also consider investing in real estate through rental properties or real estate investment trusts (REITs). If your financial goal is to save for a down payment on a house in the next five years, you may

choose to invest in less risky assets, such as high-

yield savings accounts or short-term bond funds.

Creating Passive Income Streams:

Creating passive income streams involves generating income without actively working for it. Passive income streams can come from various sources, such as rental income, dividends from stocks, or interest from bonds.

Let's say you purchase a rental property that generates $1,500 in monthly rent. After deducting expenses such as mortgage payments, property taxes, and maintenance costs, you have a net monthly income of $500. This is an example of creating passive income streams through real estate.

Another example is investing in dividend-paying stocks. Let's say you invest $10,000 in a stock that pays a 5% dividend yield. This would generate $500 in annual income, or $41.67 per month. This is an example of creating passive income streams through stocks.

Real-life cases of building wealth through investing include Warren Buffett, who is considered one of the most successful investors of all time. He built his wealth by investing in high-quality companies with a long-term growth potential. Another example is Robert Kiyosaki, the author of "Rich Dad Poor Dad," who built his wealth through investing in rental real estate. (See reference page for multiple sources on Warren Buffett and Robert Kiyosaki)

Chapter 4: Building Wealth Through Investing

In brief, investing can be a powerful tool for building long-term wealth and achieving financial independence. However, it's important to remember that the examples we've provided in this chapter are just that - examples. Before making any investments, it's crucial to thoroughly research your options and consult with a financial advisor if necessary.

Investing always comes with some level of risk, and it's essential to understand the potential risks and rewards before making any decisions. By developing an investment strategy that aligns with your financial goals, risk tolerance, and investment timeline, you can increase your chances of success in the world of investing.

Creating passive income streams can also be an effective way to build long-term wealth and achieve financial freedom. However, it's important to consider the potential tax implications and other factors before investing in any income-generating assets.

In summary, the key to successful investing is education and preparation. By understanding the basics of investing, developing a sound investment strategy, and creating passive income streams, you can put yourself on the path to financial abundance and independence. Remember to always thoroughly research your options and consult with a financial professional before making any investments.

Here's an affirmation for building wealth through investing:

"I am a savvy and successful investor, and I attract wealth and abundance through smart investment decisions. I trust in my ability to identify profitable investment opportunities and make wise decisions that generate long-term financial growth. I approach investing with a positive and proactive mindset, knowing that each investment brings me closer to achieving my financial goals. I am patient and disciplined in my investment strategies, and I focus on building a diversified portfolio that aligns with my risk tolerance and financial objectives. I am grateful for the wealth and abundance that I am creating through my investment efforts."

Chapter 5: Achieving Financial Freedom

Financial freedom is a state of being where you can live your life on your own terms without worrying about money. It's a goal that many people aspire to achieve, but it requires careful planning and hard work to make it a reality. In this chapter, we will delve into what financial freedom means and how you can attain it.

To achieve financial freedom, you need to take several steps, including creating a budget, paying off debt, saving for emergencies, and investing for the future. You must also live below your means, avoid frivolous spending, and make smart financial decisions. One way to achieve financial freedom is by increasing your income. You can do this by seeking better-paying jobs, starting a side hustle, or investing in income- generating assets.

As the old saying goes, "Money can't buy happiness, but it's a lot easier to be happy when you're not broke." So, start taking steps towards financial freedom today and enjoy the peace of mind that comes with knowing that you're in control of your financial future.

Defining Financial Freedom:

Financial freedom refers to a state where an individual has sufficient financial resources and control over their finances to lead the life they desire. It involves having enough money to cover basic needs without depending on anyone else and enough savings and investments to achieve long-term financial goals. However, financial freedom is subjective and varies from person to person based on their lifestyle, aspirations, and priorities. For some, it may mean being able to retire early and travel the world, while for others, it may simply mean having enough money to cover their day-to-day expenses without worrying about bills. Regardless of how one defines it, achieving financial freedom requires planning, budgeting, investing, and practicing financial discipline.

Steps to Achieving Financial Freedom:

1. Establish a clear financial goal: Define your financial goals, both short-term and long-term, and determine the amount of money you need to achieve them. Write them down and create a plan to achieve them.

2. Create a budget: A budget is a crucial tool in achieving financial freedom. It helps you track your income and expenses, identify areas where you can cut costs, and save money.

3. Reduce your debt: Paying off debt is a critical step in achieving financial freedom. Start by paying off high-interest debt, such as credit card debt, and work your way towards paying off other debts such as student loans or mortgages.

4. Invest wisely: Investing in assets that generate passive income can help you achieve financial

freedom. Consider stocks, bonds, or real estate that can provide you with a steady stream of income.

Maintaining Financial Independence:

Achieving financial freedom is a significant accomplishment, but it's important to remember that maintaining it requires ongoing effort. To preserve your financial independence, you must continue to practice sound financial habits such as adhering to a budget, keeping your debts in check, and making prudent investment decisions. It's also essential to have an emergency fund to fall back on in case of unexpected expenses or financial setbacks. Maintaining your financial freedom may require discipline and sacrifice, but it's worth it to ensure that you can continue to live your life on your own terms. By staying focused on your long-term goals and making smart choices, you can safeguard your financial future and enjoy the benefits of financial independence for years to come.

People who have achieved financial freedom include those who have retired early, those who have built successful businesses, and those who have made smart investment decisions. The path to financial freedom is different for everyone, but the principles remain the same: clear financial goals, budgeting, debt reduction, and smart investing. With dedication and discipline, achieving financial freedom is within reach.

Here's an affirmation for achieving

financial freedom:

"I am the master of my financial destiny, and I attract financial freedom and abundance into my life. I am committed to acting towards my financial goals and creating a life of financial security and independence. I release any limiting beliefs or negative thoughts about money, and instead, focus on the opportunities and abundance that surround me. I am resourceful and creative in finding new ways to generate income and build wealth. I am patient and disciplined in my financial strategies, knowing that each step brings me closer to achieving financial freedom. I am grateful for the financial abundance that I am creating in my life, and for the joy and freedom that comes with achieving financial independence."

Conclusion: Creating a Life of Abundance and Financial Freedom

Ultimately, creating a life of abundance and financial freedom is possible for anyone who is willing to put in the time and effort required. In this book, we've explored the importance of understanding your relationship with money, the law of attraction, practical strategies for attracting money, building wealth through investing, and achieving financial freedom.

By examining your money mindset and identifying limiting beliefs, you can begin to shift your perspective towards abundance and financial freedom. Applying the law of attraction to money can help you manifest financial abundance in your life. Practical strategies such as building a wealth consciousness, developing an abundance mentality, and taking inspired action will also help you attract more money and achieve financial independence.

Investing in assets that generate passive income is a smart way to build long-term wealth, but it's important to do your research and seek professional advice before making any decisions. And let's be honest, sometimes investing can feel like throwing a dart blindly and hoping for the best!

Achieving financial freedom requires dedication, discipline, and a willingness to learn and grow. It's important to set clear financial goals, create a budget, reduce your debt, and make smart investment decisions. Once you've achieved financial freedom, it's essential to maintain it by continuing to follow a budget, keeping your debt under control, and making wise investment decisions.

Individuals who have achieved financial freedom include entrepreneurs who have built successful businesses, investors who have made smart investment decisions, and individuals who have achieved financial independence through early retirement. While the path to financial freedom may differ for everyone, the principles remain the same: a clear financial plan, smart investments, and dedication to achieving your goals.

Achieving financial freedom requires discipline, dedication, and patience. It's not a quick fix, but it's worth it in the end. And if all else fails, you can always hope for a surprise inheritance or win the lottery! (Okay, maybe not the most practical

advice, but a little humor never hurts.)

References

Oprah Winfrey: "The Oprah Winfrey Show." YouTube, uploaded by OWN, 24 Oct. 2019, https://www.youtube.com/watch?v=7aVx6TJKh6U.

Jim Carrey: "Jim Carrey Shares His Inspiring Vision Board Story!" YouTube, uploaded by The Law of Attraction, 29 Jan. 2021, https://www.youtube.com/watch?v=rW4rvL4Fv5I.

Bob Proctor: "The Science of Getting Rich Bob Proctor" YouTube, uploaded by Quantum Leap 4 Life, 19 Feb. 2018, https://www.youtube.com/watch?v=hI-zkCmsopg.

Warren Buffett's investment strategies and success have been widely documented in various books, articles, and interviews. Here are a few sources and I recommend reading them:

"The Snowball: Warren Buffett and the Business of Life" by Alice Schroeder

"The Warren Buffett Way: Investment Strategies of the World's Greatest Investor" by Robert G. Hagstrom

"Buffett: The Making of an American Capitalist" by Roger Lowenstein

"Berkshire Hathaway's Warren Buffett: Why His Stock Picks Beat the Market" by John Reese (Forbes)

Robert Kiyosaki's success story and his real estate investment strategies have been featured in numerous interviews, articles, and books. Here are some sources and I recommend reading them:

"Rich Dad Poor Dad" by Robert Kiyosaki

"The Real Book of Real Estate" by Robert Kiyosaki

"The Millionaire Real Estate Investor" by Gary Keller, Dave Jenks, and Jay Papasan

"Robert Kiyosaki: The Millionaire Real Estate Investor" (YouTube video by Evan Carmichael)